Oscar Enrique Correa Miranda

Data processing

AF304585

Oscar Enrique Correa Miranda

Data processing

Free Software.

ScienciaScripts

Imprint

Any brand names and product names mentioned in this book are subject to trademark, brand or patent protection and are trademarks or registered trademarks of their respective holders. The use of brand names, product names, common names, trade names, product descriptions etc. even without a particular marking in this work is in no way to be construed to mean that such names may be regarded as unrestricted in respect of trademark and brand protection legislation and could thus be used by anyone.

Cover image: www.ingimage.com

This book is a translation from the original published under ISBN 978-613-9-41192-4.

Publisher:
Sciencia Scripts
is a trademark of
Dodo Books Indian Ocean Ltd. and OmniScriptum S.R.L publishing group

120 High Road, East Finchley, London, N2 9ED, United Kingdom
Str. Armeneasca 28/1, office 1, Chisinau MD-2012, Republic of Moldova, Europe
Printed at: see last page
ISBN: 978-620-8-04994-2

Copyright © Oscar Enrique Correa Miranda
Copyright © 2024 Dodo Books Indian Ocean Ltd. and OmniScriptum S.R.L publishing group

Index

Data processing is nowadays a fundamental element for everyday life, especially in universities, where it can be seen that the core activities must be based on success, progress and welfare for all members of the university community.

In this sense, it is necessary to mention, for example, the importance of the study control unit in each university, which in most cases will be in charge of receiving the enrollment of most of the students who wish to study a specific curricular unit, it is necessary to conduct surveys to make a forecast of the number of places that will be required in each curricular unit and therefore the number of professors that will be needed to teach these areas of knowledge.

It is necessary to emphasize that in every institution it is essential to demonstrate with fact the prevailing ethics and values, in that sense the responsibility in the operations that are carried out and attention to the public plays a fundamental role, since there are always the so-called hallway rumors where it is expressed informally what is really happening in each organization.

In the teaching experience, it is necessary to point out that the relationship between the teacher and the direction of control of studies is outstanding, to the extent that the enrollment of participants is properly processed and this is reflected in minutes that contain the names and data inherent to each member of the curricular unit will play a fundamental role so that the teacher has clear rules from the beginning in the classroom, This means that it is essential that all teachers have in their hands at the beginning of student activities all those who are truly enrolled, and who do not have priority problems with respect to the formal studies to be carried out.

In this sense, reference should be made to the importance of the relationship between the internal client who works in the control of studies and the external client, which in this case would be represented by the students, who obviously manage a kind of informal indicators that are focused on the quality of service. In this sense, it is necessary to emphasize that if the student feels that he/she was properly attended to and that he/she was able to register in the expected time for a given semester of his/her career, it is obviously something that will be in his/her comfort zone and perhaps will not point it out as something important, However, when it is observed that there is a failure in the processing of this information, either because the student was not informed in time or because the formal registration was simply not completed, then obviously, in an informal or formal manner, the perspective is focused on discouragement or a bad feeling of having been inefficiently attended to.

Therefore it is necessary to emphasize that the management of information in any organization is fundamental, taking into consideration the time plays a valuable role when carrying out the activities, in order to inform the related parties either the internal customer represented by those who provide the service in the institution or the external customer which in this case is all those students who need to fulfill their academic activities in the time they have longed for their lives.

It is necessary to have processors and computers that allow at the beginning to keep a record of the number of participants who wish to enroll in a given semester, obviously all this must be stored in a database that must have a backup to ensure that at the end the teacher can have the report card based on an effective enrollment by students.

So it can be seen that data processing, storage capacity, information backup and timely delivery of information to the parties involved play a fundamental role in today's institutions.

At the beginning, it is possible to count on the available data that may be the intention of a participant focused on enrolling a specific curricular unit, taking into consideration the relevant conditional of the priority, which guarantees that every person who studies at university can count on a continuation of his/her studies where the logic of knowledge is efficiently assimilated, from the cognitive and cognitive point of view of the participant.

In summary, it can be seen that the capacity to respond in an institution will be linked to the technology available and the willingness of people to use it effectively. Data processing in an institution from the perspective of total quality will definitely guarantee the continuous improvement of processes.

In this sense, inspections can be carried out to verify the level of compliance with an objective on a given date, making the necessary corrective actions in case of observing any type of limitation or failure that is present, and obviously in the case of detecting in any process that the goal is being achieved, the enthusiasm and will must be kept well focused to continue obtaining positive results over time, understanding perfectly that at every moment new ideas can be integrated to improve what has already been developed in a timely manner.

Source: Correa O, 2024. Data processing.

It is necessary to understand the importance of data collection in any organization, which is reflected in something as simple as the initial class in any curricular unit in which there is a classroom protocol, which invites participants to make themselves known is the so-called individual presentation, which is a form of brief interview but that will allow the group and especially the facilitator of the curricular unit to understand the interests and motivations of each participant in order to effectively guide the knowledge to be transmitted throughout the semester of class.

Now, once this initial presentation is completed, the learning contract is made known, which represents the possibility for the student to know the activities to be carried out, the strategies and the date to deliver all these evaluations. This will allow the activities to generate a kind of confidence because the rules are clear, but it also allows the participant to keep an effective control of how many activities he/she has been able to accomplish up to a certain date, in order to understand what should be emphasized or what aspects should be improved.

In the teaching practice it is necessary to indicate the importance of remembering the activities to be achieved during the curricular unit, for this purpose, presenting the assignments in a blog or web page can play a fundamental role, so that the student has clarity of everything that is to be achieved and understands that it has a logic that relates the contents to a final objective.

In this scenario, it is necessary to highlight the importance that processors play nowadays, since most of the participants use their smartphones to access the multimedia contents that are dictated in each university lecture. There are cases of teachers who are even studying at doctoral level using their smartphones to write the different assignments they have had to complete at some point.

When referring to the doctoral level, virtual classes are normally executed under the modality of the implementation of scripts or online programs such as Moodle or Google classroom, which allow the facilitator to clearly establish the units to be fulfilled and the participants, in this case the doctoral students, the obligation and duty to fulfill each of these assignments in order to qualify for a doctoral level academic degree.

In most cases they usually use eight-core processors which have 3 GB of RAM for efficient performance in the activities of writing text, making presentations, developing calculations.

On the other hand, there are those who prefer to use the traditional way of the desktop computer, which currently can be used on average an i5 computer that has four physical cores, sixth generation in which you can work various computer programs for data processing and internet connection as browsers.

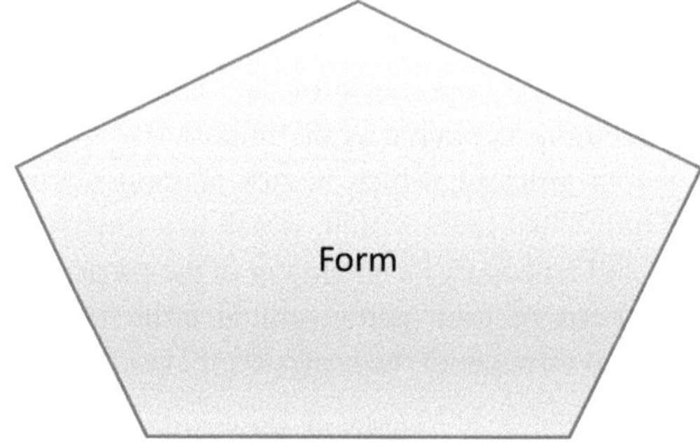

Source: Correa O, 2024. Form.

When talking about data processing it is necessary to understand that it has a structure normally established through the hardware, which definitely receives life or utility when a program normally known as software is installed in that point at present also refer to technology equipment that have eight processors, which are represented in the ninth generation i7 computers normally used for high-end games.

Definitely, when teaching a curricular unit linked to data processing, it is totally valid to generate forms that can be programmed in i7 computers, which will allow to organize and present the data in an adequate way. In this sense it is necessary to indicate that nowadays it is possible to connect HTML CSS technology with JavaScript, in order to generate dynamic environments that allow students to have access to a program to enter their data or simply express their willingness to enroll in a particular curricular unit.

In the case of social networks they are definitely wonderful examples of effective data processing at a global level, trying to build a social network at this time is a wonderful journey but from the point of view of computer programming with high-level languages today is an opportunity to acquire new programming skills to those previously existing.

Definitely to try to accomplish a feat of such magnitude as being able to create from home a social network that has a global impact, it is necessary at first with such a fundamental power supply that gives 24 hours a day guarantee of its use both from the level of programming and from the level of the external client, which in this case is represented by the users.

In this sense it is necessary to talk about the back end, which will ensure to have the infrastructure and data necessary to realize a project as important as a social network, for this schedule a dedicated server 24 hours a day is a fundamental element, which must be supported on a source of energy preferably renewable in this regard there are alternatives such as windmills that are currently being widely used.

But definitely one of the great challenges at this time is to generate these processes of sustainability in the systems that are desired to present globally, for this the initiative of developing a tesla coil that supports computational processes comes to be a truly brilliant idea that represents a journey quite important but really worth a try.

It is necessary to remember that great scientists like Nikola Tesla who in his time had the vision of an integrated world, which could be supported by free energy and that today makes sense to try to give sustainability to isolated processes to servers that allow access to customers around the world and can enjoy an optimal service that is stable, thanks to that vision to generate educational processes that are self-sustaining where you can integrate power generation technology infrastructure based on servers with internet connection and Wi-Fi systems, in order to generate optimal results to users globally.

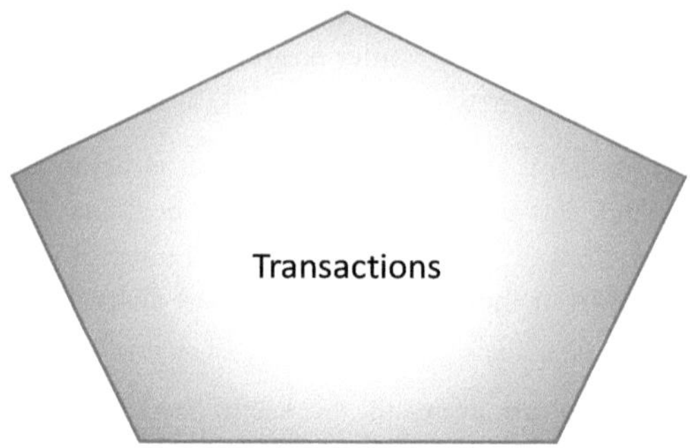

Source: Correa O, 2024. Transactions.

Nowadays it is wonderful to observe how many social networks through the so-called hyperlinks can integrate processes on a global scale, which in turn can be linked to financial processes. It is necessary to emphasize that in social networks the incorporation of the so-called virtual payment cards is a modality that currently represents a competitive advantage at a global level for most people.

Every day more and more people want to carry out activities from their homes and for this purpose they use the so-called virtual financial transactions as forms of transactions, which every day incorporate new security and verification systems to provide customers with the greatest possible security and satisfaction.

From the perspective of developing projects that integrate social networks that connect to financial systems at a global level, represent a challenge that from the programming level is quite interesting to meet, for this there are currently technologies such as the so-called i9 processors which can have up to 18 cores incorporated, in order to ensure the multiprocessing so necessary today to generate an optimal result for all parties.

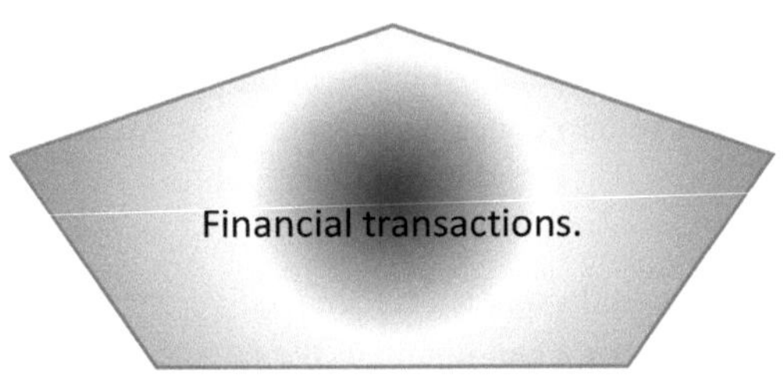

Source: Correa O, 2024. Financial transactions.

Currently it is important to understand that when talking about data processing there are video accelerator cards also known as GPUs, graphics processing units come to facilitate the opportunity to work with design programs such as AutoCAD, which can generate models that are useful for mechanical processes, for example. In this type of system you can easily draw vehicles or robot prototypes that come to perform a practical activity in real life, often you can combine the part of the design locally on the computer, depending on the marketing that can be connected in turn with the Internet to represent certain activities that are connected with the automotive sector or the development of robots for manufacturing companies.

So obviously the design of these graphics often requires higher capabilities than a traditional processor that is going to take care of the general management of the computer, such processors have been evolving since the last century until today and today it is visualized that they can have more than 18 integrated cores to generate a truly significant power.

But obviously there are times when it is necessary to devote computer resources especially in the area of design or graphics generation, at that time will intervene the GPU cards which may be focused on improving the performance of a program in terms of speed and definition of images, in the case of the generation of designs of cars or robots, it may be necessary to use and implement this type of card to improve not only the performance of the program that is being used for design but also to obtain final results that are optimal.

It is necessary to understand that the field of action of the GPU is extremely broad today, they can contribute significantly in the development of activities focused on artificial intelligence. In that sense, when making reference to financial transactions nowadays we can observe the incorporation of artificial intelligence systems to web systems or internet sites, in that sense we can find the so-called virtual robots that are assistants that bring a series of predefined answers and can interact in real time with people accessing the technological systems belonging to online banking.

Obviously at the financial level, it is currently required to provide real-time response to multiple users, who access to perform various transactions in real time 24 hours a day to online banking. In that sense, to speak of quality in the provision of service from the Internet, not only wants to take into consideration robots or Android that can interact with users but also transactions that allow you to feel reliable in real time to subscribers of bank accounts.

Every bank customer today understands the imperative need to carry out their transactions online, among them we can highlight the payment of services, electronic transfers, receipt of money and request for certificates, among others.

In this sense it is necessary to understand that currently many of these systems are hosted on servers that work with the cloud, to be able to store large amounts of information reliably. In this sense, the incorporation of a GPU card, higher than 1750 MHz, a bandwidth of 448 GB/s, may represent the possibility of giving greater functionality to the client-server relationship taking into consideration an internet transmission speed that is quite acceptable today for the requirements of online banking customers.

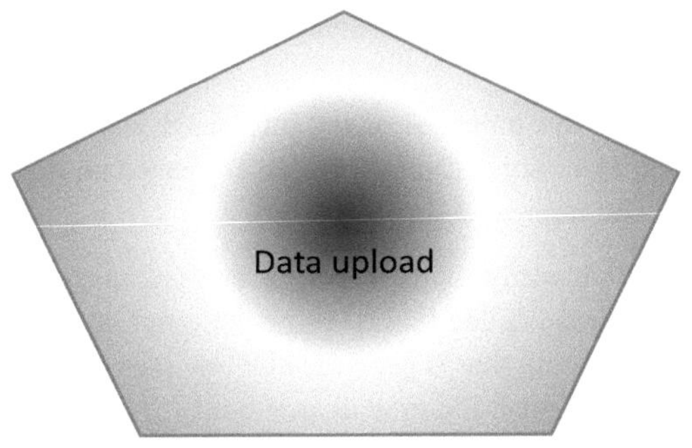

Source: Correa O, 2024. Data upload.

Nowadays, the use of GPU cards, also known as graphic processing units, is highly recommended, in which thousands or millions of transistors are integrated in order to carry out an activity related to the development of information technology.

It is necessary to indicate in this sense that there are Internet portals that have servers that store their information in the cloud, which is practically equivalent to almost infinite storage capacity, this has had the advantage that thousands or millions of subscribers can connect simultaneously to achieve a wonderful online interaction, which is currently focused on the online generation of images or videos that can be stored and downloaded on these servers.

In this sense, it can be observed how the storage capacity at a global level has increased, which has brought as a consequence that in those Internet sites that contain those servers as a fundamental base for the practically limited storage of information, it is possible to achieve an interaction between people at a global level that reaches the point of forming different topics of interest in the field of information technology.

It is necessary to highlight that this type of servers can incorporate these GPU cards, which can take full advantage of the transmission capacity of the Internet, so that users can quickly create their images or videos to improve the Internet connection, but also the processing speed of the activities that are running online.

And we are currently seeing that many of these servers are connected to other social networks through the so-called links and hyperlinks, in order to generate interaction processes that truly generate a transcendental motivation in various areas of life, be it medicine, education or simply video games.

Most artificial intelligence platforms can integrate the potential of GPU cards in their servers, in order to achieve the processing capacity so necessary to generate the new interactive dialogues, images or videos required by users around the world on these platforms.

At this point, we must imagine the potential of the integrated vision of the Internet, where we speak of enhanced electronic searches, which are based on the fundamental characteristic of continuous and improved learning.

It is necessary to emphasize that many of these platforms that surely integrate these video and internet processing cards, called GPUs, allow the programs to generate such a fundamental process as the learning that is generated by the interaction with a certain user, who obviously in most cases must log in with an e-mail.

For more than 40 years now there has been talk of the application of artificial intelligence, which could generate a kind of decontrol at the moment when they become self-aware and organize themselves to maintain control over all processes on planet Earth.

Well, what decades ago was simply pure science fiction, today for many scientists represents a truly interesting topic of debate, which obviously has an important impact on the development of public safety.

Today, for example, there is talk of the development of robots focused on public safety, which surely using a Wi-Fi connection system allow them to have a real interaction with the processes that must be performed in order to maintain effective security for all citizens of a given city.

In that sense, beyond the scientific debate or fear that has been presented in science fiction movies, it is observed that this type of systems already have built-in facial recognition, which can allow it to interact effectively with the user who is trying to access or connect to the system.

Obviously, it is necessary to say that a process of global warming is currently taking place on planet Earth, which has been gradually increasing since the so-called Industrial Revolution, in which industrial processes were automated, often forgetting the imminent environmental consequences.

But beyond that when talking about the environment we have to make reference to the multiple factors involved, the processes of deforestation on a global scale have also unfortunately come to mark a situation in which the planet earth is not allowed to regenerate as it should, in this scenario that is being developed, hypothetically these artificial intelligence systems through the use of androids could get to perform activities in environments or climates that may exceed what is acceptable at the biological level, So beyond the fear for the use or development of self-awareness in artificial intelligence systems, we must think about the opportunity we have right now to begin to implement such systems in areas where you want to conduct research such as in the deep sea, very high mountains or areas that are truly inaccessible due to their climate.

Based on all these arguments then it is necessary to say that we must welcome all these systems that together with the GPU cards, which were initially used for everything related to the development of graphics and video games, today has been expanding to be used at the level of artificial intelligence systems that have as fundamental characteristic not only its interaction with the user with the person who asks a question or concern, but also has the ability to learn based on the questions and answers that simultaneously is generating the system in a matter of seconds.

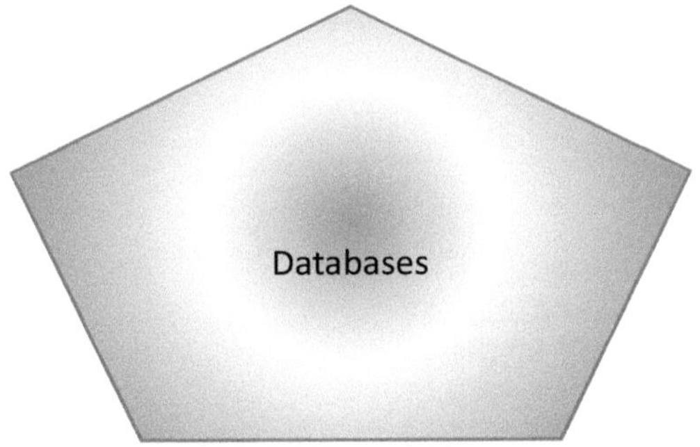

Source: Correa O, 2024. Database.

In the field of information storage it is necessary to disclose that GPU cards are going to interact with cloud servers, in most cases such websites that are dedicated to provide service focused on the development of artificial intelligence allow the user to have an account through their email.

This has a significant advantage since, as search results are generated or simply generating new images or video, a history of the activities performed can be kept. It is important to highlight the importance of the so-called prompts, which are instructions that can be easily recognized by artificial intelligence systems.

There are simple prompts that can be instructions that are intended for the generation of an image that is made from the perspective of artificial intelligence, usually this procedure is characterized at first in the search for images that have to do with what the user wants, once found it proceeds to give a result that is transformed by the internal vision where obviously the speed of the GPU card will generate a fundamental role to obtain an optimal result in terms of image definition and overall presentation of the details that are desired in the final format.

It is necessary to point out that most of the websites that provide these services have these GPU cards, which give a very outstanding performance to obtain a quite acceptable final product.

Now, it is necessary to understand that the user who is interacting with these servers that are supported by state-of-the-art technology, does not necessarily have to have a GPU card, but if he is interacting from a computer that has a Gigahertz processor, he will obviously feel that he is not getting the results he wants in the desired time.

At this point it is recommended from the user's perspective to interact at least from a system that has a quad-core processor, above 2 GHz so that the user's perspective and use is optimal and the results are obtained in a naturally acceptable time.

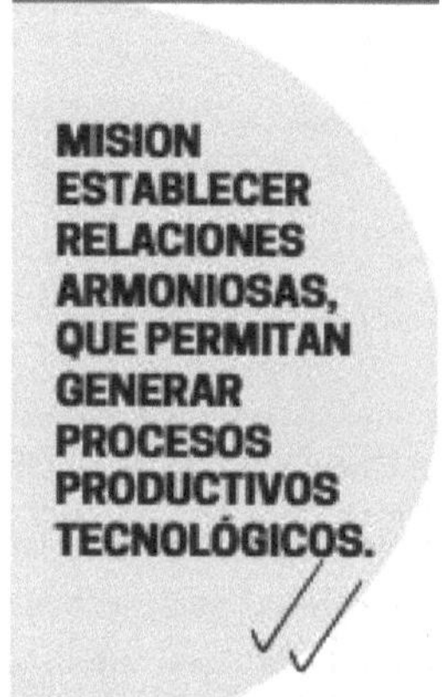

Source: Correa O, 2024. Mission.

It is necessary to indicate that in function of a kind of data processing the use of a GPU card, in a computer becomes fundamental, since there are cases in which you want to generate dialogues with moving images that often synchronize the words with the gestures, obviously all this has reached the point of appearing to have so much realism that many social networks already include in their policies of use that all people who are going to upload some kind of video that is related or supported in artificial intelligence preferably this is marked as created by artificial intelligence.

In this sense, there are synthetic voices that can be incorporated into an image which, by respecting ethics and values and being in function of supporting education, can be very well seen by most social networks, to the point of not only being accepted from the point of view of monetization or the possibility of generating money with that audiovisual content, but also in many cases receives a transcendental acceptance by users in general of social networks.

Obviously, today it is possible to generate characters called avatars, which can express gestures and movements according to a content that normally with a synthesized voice can be generated to create an audiovisual impact around a specific topic.

In the case of the generation of avatars with movement obviously requires the incorporation of GPU cards in a computer and programs that when installed can be executed by a user who must follow instructions in some cases of programming and in others simply object-oriented design. In the case of data processing today there are programs that, when incorporated into the computer, can generate designs that work in virtual and mixed reality.

In the case of data processing it makes a lot of sense to give classes under these mixed technology schemes, for example, if you are trying to explain the characteristics of a GPU which often incorporate thousands or millions of transistors, at first you can show through the webcam that is connected to the computer that physical artifact. Then you can work digitally with the possibility of emphasizing the texture or drawings that are necessary to explain the possibilities of adaptation and improvement to artificial intelligence processes that have today's GPU cards.

In that sense to generate a learning process around data processing can get to incorporate the camera to show the GPU card, while in the internal design of the program can be placed images or texture that rotate in three dimensions to explain in various perspectives both virtual and real As a process can influence in this case for the improvement of performance and final product of what you want to achieve.

It is necessary to point out that in an introductory data processing class, although it is true that traditional computer concepts are fundamental, it is also necessary to point out that most students have a preference for the use of intelligent cellular systems technology.

At this point the knowledge facilitator has to try to get into the development of applications that may be of interest to the participants, using artificial intelligence with images that are eye-catching and topical.

Definitely when referring to a class focused on data processing also using virtual and mixed reality, for example, the camera can focus on what is a phone and text editing programs that have, while in the virtual reality environment can be explained the advantages of using this type of technology and telephony in terms of writing a text or a special work of degree.

When teaching a data processing class using virtual and mixed reality, which is traditionally worked on from a computer with a quad-core processor, it can often seem to the student that he may be distant from it or that the technology is simply unattainable.

And it is not that it is out of reach, but simply that most young people today are preferably linked or related to the technology of smartphones which are very fast and very safe to use. So their preference and acceptability is traditionally greater than that of a computer that we have known since the 20th century.

In some cases the student feels limited to see that the facilitator is using a computer especially if they do not have such a device at home, however, it is necessary to indicate that many of these computer programs have been updated and improved for the technology of smart phone systems and are available from the app store that can be downloaded from Android or iOS systems.

At that moment it is up to the facilitator of the curricular unit introduction to data processing to generate that positive interaction with the participant that should be at first informative, and it should be understood that the participant may have a focus more towards smart telephony but it does not mean that he cannot appropriate the design and generation of new programs or software with the use of his phone simply by using the virtual and mixed technology editing tools that are available from the applications that can be downloaded and installed on most people's phones.

Young people can definitely present a very high vocation for curricular units linked to data processing, obviously they know what represents a content that is useful and topical since the internet and social networks are constantly informing about courses or programs that are relevant in the field of Artificial Intelligence.

There are traditional programs or applications such as WhatsApp that should be a fundamental part of a class focused on the introduction to data processing, which most students either by a family or friend situation has such an application on their phones.

At this point it is necessary to understand the importance of creating groups in social networks to integrate the participants, being necessary to emphasize that the facilitator today must have a focus and a vocation almost daily around learning new approaches and knowledge that arise in the technological area.

In some cases students refer to online artificial intelligence systems, which have direct competence in the field of data processing as they allow editing text or images online and can be downloaded to the computer or phone.

In this sense, it is advisable that the facilitator of the curricular unit of data processing has an open approach to new paradigms or websites that are emerging on the Internet, especially when a virtual class is taught, it is necessary to understand that there are participants who have previous knowledge about how to make videos with artificial intelligence, images or intelligent text editing.

At that moment the facilitator has a wonderful opportunity to overcome some kind of personal gap in the learning that he/she has, it is necessary to understand that in the era or social knowledge we all have some grain of sand to contribute in terms of data processing.

But it is necessary to have humility to understand that, just as artificial intelligence systems are constantly generating a learning process very similar to our neuronal system. We also have to have a firm vocation to generate a self-learning process that adapts to current needs and requirements.

Artificial intelligence systems philosophically assume the position of having the ability to learn based on the interaction they have with their users through questions or answers, definitely also the facilitator of introduction to data processing has the fundamental responsibility to have the necessary humility.

To understand that at some point a student's knowledge or a topic that is unknown may arise, but having the vocation to assimilate and understand it can overcome the learning gaps and demonstrate to the student body that they have a person who is able to listen to them and adapt these new technologies to the teaching and learning process that is being managed.

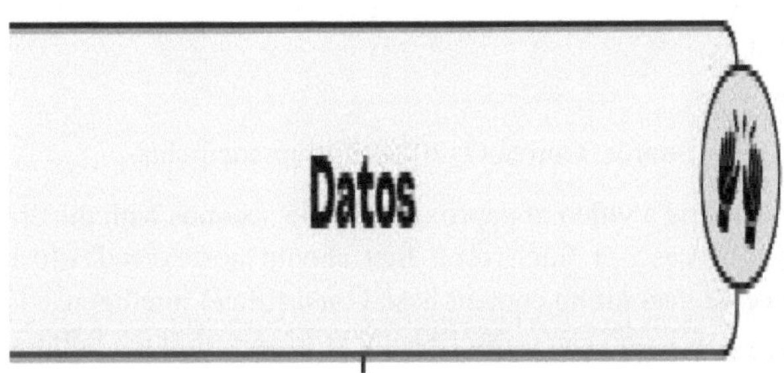

Source: Correa O, 2024. Data.

The time may come when it is necessary to incorporate a GPU card to a computer, in the process of teaching data processing is necessary to emphasize that artificial intelligence programs are constantly being updated which will represent that you must have a greater amount of significant storage to be able to integrate these updates effectively that obviously come to give greater functionality to what you are trying to do as a final result.

In the case of the use of programs that develop artificial intelligence, we can highlight the importance of some of them, which basically by dictating a word or a phrase have the ability to develop images that are linked to a specific topic, in this way, nowadays videos can be generated that are longer than 5 minutes where texts that have been created at some point through artificial intelligence are combined with images, obviously in many of these cases the final result or multimedia file can have a weight of more than 650 mb of storage.

The size of the final result will obviously depend on the type of resolution that is desired in some cases when working with a resolution higher than 4k, it is necessary to understand that the image will have a higher definition but it is also necessary to have more storage capacity locally on the hard disk.

Which in turn also has to be understood that depending on what is the hosting of the information should require greater data transmission capacity on the Internet. There are certain cases in which you can generate a multimedia content based on artificial intelligence taking into consideration a low image quality that is traditionally known in such programs as the draft, in that sense the difference with respect to a video that is developed in the field of 4k can be quite considerable.

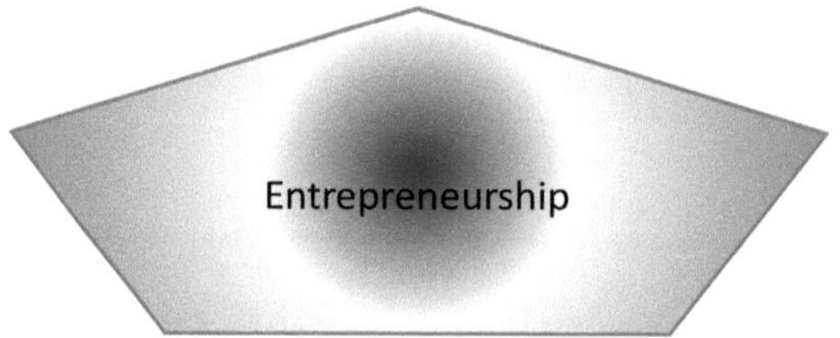

Source: Correa O, 2024. Entrepreneurship.

In the case of generating a video of approximately 45 seconds with the draft format can be obtained in most cases a final result that should not exceed 140 megabytes of storage.when you are generating content based on artificial intelligence is necessary to indicate that many times you can transcribe a text to appear at the bottom of the video, which directly affects the process of visual appeal that you want to get, but also in the engagement or ability to attract the attention of the end user which is really what you always want.

Once you have placed the written text in the different sections of the images that are part of the video, you can proceed to assign what is a synthetic voice that traditionally will express what is contained as its title in the video. This type of Synthetic Voices can vary in terms of female or male style, but also in terms of much lower or less high-pitched tones.

This transcription of text that can be pronounced by artificial voices has reached a really interesting point, you can select voices of people with different accents which can vary according to their nationality. Even this has reached the point where the speed of pronunciation of the synthetic voice that is being reproduced can be made faster or slower, everything will depend on the needs of the final audience to be captivated.

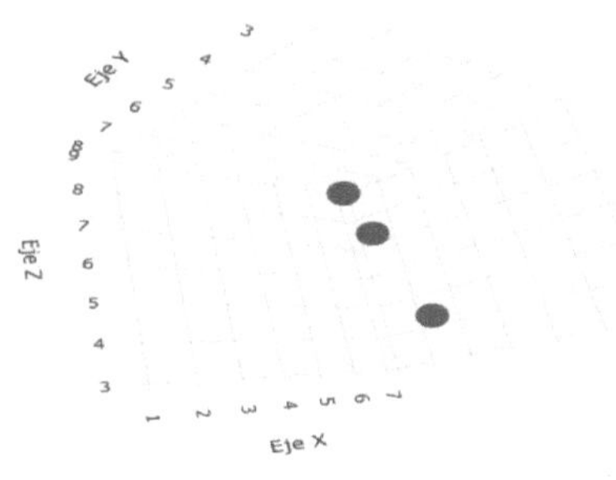

Source: Correa O, 2024. Three-dimensional graphic

Some artificial intelligence programs when installed on a computer may require a GPU card, since in some cases these programs have the ability to generate effects to the designs of the images that are being presented, one of the most common and used is the combination of images with videos that appear to be integrated and unified as one.

In practice, for example, this means that in the upper part of the video a fixed image is established, and in the lower part, what would be a car moving along a highway appears, showing not only the traffic signs of the road but also the nature and the sky to generate a contrast of movement, but also enhancing the upper image that is desired to have as a priority.

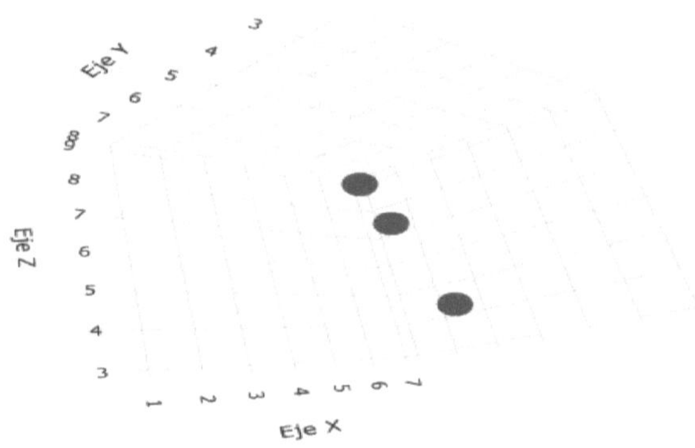

Source: Correa O, 2024. Three-dimensional graphic

It should be noted that a statistical analysis of indicators focused on data processing can currently be carried out. Definitely, when indicators are mentioned, it should be taken into consideration that they represent the capacity to analyze the current state of a situation to be evaluated, but they can also be taken into consideration 5 years before or 5 years after the current reality.

In this sense, when referring to this fascinating world of indicators focused on data processing, we must take into consideration the current prevailing technological strengths, most of which are based on the Internet, taking into consideration artificial intelligence systems that run their activities on servers that simulate a cloud of information, normally known as cloud servers.

Obviously in an information society where searches are constantly made, but also new knowledge is created through the generation of images, videos and graphics, it is necessary to say or point out at that moment that it must have an important capacity to be able to store all that information that is constantly being generated.

That is why these servers called in the cloud, are now playing an important role to the point that many companies are engaged in providing storage rental service which in principle can vary from 5 GB to an unlimited storage possibility also known in some cases as Hosting.

Faced with this situation there are comparative advantages and disadvantages to be analyzed, among the main advantages is to have a company that is active 24 hours a day providing a storage service that through a password and a user should store a series of information that is uploaded simultaneously to the servers traditionally taking Internet protocols based on navigation within browsers.

This point should refer to self-service on demand, which is the possibility that the end user who needs a hosting or site to store information, has the possibility of uploading his information in real time without the need for a third party to intervene in the process. In this sense it is necessary to emphasize that the so-called file transfer protocol, also known since the 20th century as ftp, is still in force, which is a secure way that through a graphical interface allows the user to have a double screen.

The main screen comes to represent all those files that you are managing on your computer or smartphone, second screen would be focused on the remote directory or destination folder in which to host all those files that need to be backed up either by security measure or as a simple way to have the information remotely available 24 hours a day.

This situation is necessary to say that several companies have emerged globally that have large storage capacities which surely have these GPU cards, which allow to expand the speed of processing and connection in the processes to the Internet.

Obviously as for this service the fundamental thing that is required is above all things that it is available both in downloading and uploading in a relatively short time or preferably in a matter of seconds. The advantage of this type of self-service with cloud-based servers, is that they give the user the possibility of having the information they need to have in an immediate way, it is necessary to point out the case for example of the thesis of degree many times it is observed that the participants when they are making the different chapters of their research work can find that it takes a number of weeks of research and dedication to transcribe on your computer, which obviously presented a number of vulnerabilities especially at the time that the hard drive of the computer arises some failure that is serious and that does not really allow recovering the information.

At that moment the backup service that has been obtained from a cloud server comes into action, since, if the student has managed to upload daily updates related to his thesis to the cloud server, then simply once he has repaired his hard disk the only thing he will have to do is download it to continue working on the last chapter he has uploaded to the storage server.

Faced with this situation there are those who say that there could be vulnerabilities when hiring this type of cloud services in a private company, because many times there are terms of service where the company in theory should provide a service 24 hours a day in reality that does not happen, so various changes can occur including vulnerability in the security of systems that leads to that at some point even a private company providing such a service has some kind of failure that is temporary or indefinite.

Therefore, the information must be backed up in at least two storage units, since even those systems with international backup units in international servers can fail, causing important losses in the information. Facing this dilemma obviously raises the situation in which the user who is processing data or simply is transcribing his thesis, may think about the possibility of transforming your computer or laptop in a cloud-style storage system to ensure backup of information to their own processes.

Obviously, in the context of this current situation, it would be necessary to highlight an indicator in the use of data processing that is basically focused on the level of information backup, which in practice, due to all the vulnerabilities mentioned above, must be supported by three different and independent sources of information storage.

In this sense, depending on the level of importance of the information, it is possible to talk about an indicator of information backup supported by a high level of quality, which should consist, from the administrative and managerial point of view, in the possibility that the institution or company that is being managed can effectively count on free private cloud servers that allow immediate availability of the key information handled, and that this is a fundamental complement to all the processes that are stored in the institution's computers.

This indicator would then be composed of three fundamental parts, the first two based on the use of cloud services both from private companies and free services, which must be updated prudently from the institution's servers. Since nowadays the information that is handled is key and many times can be confidential, it is also required that there is a trained staff in this area to ensure that these processes are met effectively.

Not only from a supervisory point of view, but also from a statistical point of view, that is to say, a record must be kept of the information handled within the institution and everything that has already been backed up, so as to never leave to chance something that could be key to the development of the institution's processes.

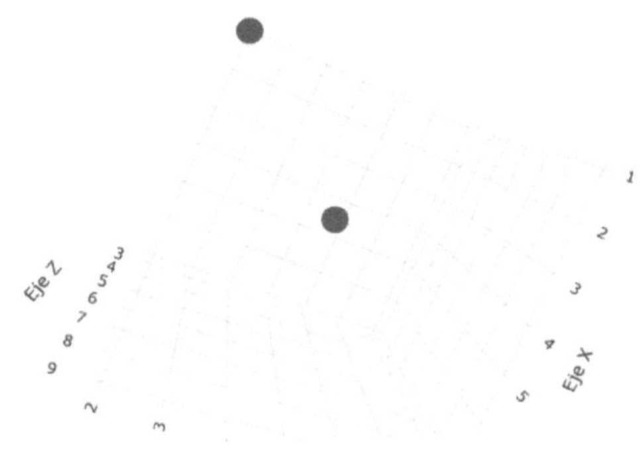

Source: Correa O, 2024. Indicators.

In the case of university institutions it is well known that the professor's activity can be focused on teaching, research and university extension. But even in any of these processes it is necessary to keep a record of the activities that are done, especially when interacting with university students. In this sense, in the teaching part, indicators must be managed, which are normally associated with the possibility of evaluating the final performance of each student, through the assignment of a final grade.

In this sense, in the case of universities with national characteristics that have a presence in the territory of a country as a whole, it is necessary for the central level to establish systems that have the possibility of connecting in real time with the different sites of the university in order to have a reliable registry, preferably uploaded from the teaching level.

In this sense, three fundamental factors come into play, based on the main nucleus of the university, which must have the necessary databases and servers to store all this information in the form of notes. As a second important point, it should be taken into consideration that the study control level of each university site should have central access to be able to upload the list of participants and open the possibility for each professor of the curricular units to upload their grades at the end of the course, either from home or from a computer room belonging to the institution.

Speaking of indicator management from the point of view of data processing at the macro level in universities, the average time taken to upload grades should be taken into consideration. For this purpose, a record should be kept of all the professors at the national level who were able to upload grades on time, which in the end is an advantage for the students, since if any curricular unit has priority, the necessary precautions could be taken at that point.

To improve this indicator of effectiveness in the uploading of grades, it is obviously necessary from the central level of the university to generate the necessary and relevant information regarding the beginning of the uploading of grades by the teaching level and the end, it should clearly reflect the initial date on which each teacher can upload the grade of their students and the end in which they must print the report and send it to the central level of the university so that all these data can be processed and represent reliable information for the welfare of all students and the harmonious development of the university.

The teaching experience indicates that the participants can determine almost instantaneously from a visual inspection process if any curricular unit can meet their expectations or interests, in that sense they usually intuitively analyze the level of actuality of the contents that the facilitator is teaching and if they really feel that it is in accordance with the reality that they know in their smart phone and all the programs they use then they take the next step, which is to begin to deliver their activities in the corresponding time.

This motivation on the part of the student will influence an extremely important indicator that can also motivate the performance of the facilitator. In this sense, the level of permanence of the student in the activity of the curricular unit should be mentioned; in order to analyze this indicator, 100% of the students who began to visualize or approach the first class should be taken into account, and how many of them were able to finish their last evaluation in the estimated time span.

At this point it is necessary to indicate that this indicator cannot include all those students who decided to enroll in the curricular unit and who appear on the list; only those students on the class list who attended the first activity and were able to successfully complete the proposed activities, which traditionally can be five evaluations in the case of a university curricular unit, should be taken into account for the evaluation of this indicator.

It is necessary to say that many times there is the need to update the laboratories in the universities to be able to have the computer programs that are really at the forefront, when these situations do not occur in the experience it is observed that there are professors with a great initiative that have invested in technology.

Either in Tablet phones, laptops or computers, and that these resources are made available to students not in a direct way in terms of physical contact, but also develop websites, blogs or applications that allow participants to have access to all that knowledge that the teacher has managed to develop from home but that represents an innovation for all of them.

At that moment we would be in the presence of a facilitator of a curricular unit with a fundamental characteristic which is the capacity for self-learning and the fundamental motivation to make quality content available to his students so that they also feel highly satisfied.

Definitely in the university processes regarding the backup of information in the cloud, taking this indicator based on this external support, both private and free, plus the internal technological management of each university is something that allows every university to have greater control over this important issue such as the grade of each student, which after all has to lead to the graduation of a professional who is responsible based on values and who with his knowledge can contribute to a better society and a better planet.

Now as an indicator of the performance of a teacher today, when it is observed that this professional is working in a classroom or from home through a virtual platform or social network, but has the ability to incorporate their personal resources to give greater importance to what is being taught, then it can be referred to a facilitator who fulfills all the desired university and personal values and becomes an example to follow within the university.

And this is reflected in practice at the time when the teacher is called to attend a promotion course, which normally can be a very favorable initiative for all teachers at a university because if they are given a course, for example, at doctoral level and they have to comply with a series of activities in order to pass it plus a final presentation of a degree thesis, that point then we could speak of the litmus test for outstanding teaching staff.

In the course of these activities of professional improvement through the exhibitions, each of the teachers must demonstrate how within their professorships they have been developing activities that contribute to the development of society, to allow a society that includes environmental values and respect, but also that allows others to be much more productive from the research that is being developed from the university cluster.

This promotion course can be called the so-called test of fire because there comes a time when a professional staff is formed that will in turn evaluate the teachers, and at that time obviously takes into consideration the degree work that each of them are presenting and depending on the classification obtained so they in turn may make a final presentation where you can truly evaluate the ability of each teacher to incorporate their own technological resources, This is a self-training process that effectively contributes to the development of their curricular unit, but above all, to know how to disseminate using the current information technology, whether it is a script application, a web page, a blog or simply social networks.

A university professor complies with all this process in his evaluation for a promotion to a higher category scale, then we could refer to a professional who has devoted his life to teaching, research and university extension, highlighting even from his university having global projection, standing out among many professionals to demonstrate that the quality of service is what prevails when innovation is present as a fundamental marrow and the vocation of service to others as a personal way of life.

It is necessary to indicate that reference is made to the importance of being able to count on cloud storage services, which take into consideration external sources such as private companies or institutions that offer the service free of charge in order to leverage the internal management that is performed from the main server of the institution with this double control.

The fulfillment of these three factors would denote a fairly acceptable level of information management. From the point of view of the information backup indicator, certain fundamental steps would be fulfilled in order to provide the possibility that at some point in time, if any of these elements fail, two others would still be available and could come into operation to respond to the information needs that may be required at some point in time.

However, it should be taken into consideration that the information backup indicator is acceptable in principle, but like any other institution, the indicators should still be within the framework of total quality management or continuous improvement, understanding that even from a practical perspective, the management and backup of information is quite acceptable.

With this triad mentioned above, one must always have an eye on the concept of technological independence to give a better performance to all those indicators that from the practical vision are acceptable but always from the theory and dreams that every business leader has to have in his mind can be effective with the use of technological development implemented progressively.

In this sense, in order to enhance those information storage indicators that at some point may be acceptable, it is necessary to deepen the concept of technological independence within the organization to begin to develop and implement servers that are powered by the traditional electrical energy that comes from the supply that all state institutions provide through electricity grids, which in theory should always work incorrectly state should think much further should begin to generate those technologies that contribute to implement new energy processes within each institution.

It is important to highlight the integration of multidisciplinary teams in which the people who develop the system area also have contact with all those who at some point may develop some type of research for the generation of electric energy.

In this sense, to begin to establish projects focused on the development of windmills that take advantage of the wind, the development of motors that enhance the generation of energy, the development of tesla coil designs that allow any institution to dream of energy independence through research, is something that from the point of view of total quality management and the leadership of any institution should be kept in mind.

Obviously, the integration of a multidisciplinary team will play a fundamental role so that all those projects that are being developed in the energy area will provide effective and substantial support to those processors that have a cloud-style approach, so that at that moment we can also have the possibility of having an internal service that stores a large amount of information storage, and that is backed up by traditional sources of electricity generation as well as those being generated within the institution.

In this sense, it can be considered that the inspection is fulfilled because it has what is available in the market and internally in the institution, take into consideration the quality control because statistical results are taken into consideration of how much information has been stored in number of gigabytes or megabytes and how much space will be needed for the next two years at least, taking into consideration the medium term as something quite valid for example to manage the study control management in a university.

Quality assurance is when all these manuals are taken into account, which in some way are recorded on a daily basis, which are presented weekly in graphical forms in order to visually understand how each of the processes are being carried out in the system area and how this in turn can be interrelated with the area of energy research to effectively contribute in the long term of 5 years to the energy and technological independence that every university must have.

Contributing to a dream of this magnitude thanks to the efforts of a team of multidisciplinary professionals should ultimately have an impact on the creation of this total quality management, in which the impulse of leadership is based on the possibility of not only complying with international process standardization norms, but also of managing.

To manage the processes from the vision of technological independence to understand that all those forms of measurement of the processes of information management and control of information, become armored when there is strength in the heart to develop energy and server technologies to have adequate storage, which in turn allows processing data on time in this case to have a record for example of something as important as the level of passes in each curriculum unit, or simply the level of students who manage to successfully complete a particular career.

This whole world of data processing indicator management becomes fascinating when there is the will to integrate efforts through a common goal that leads to generate the necessary technological and energetic empowerment, to demonstrate with examples that the University research carried out in a given institution is giving effective results, and that it has the necessary motivation to overcome all obstacles.

Just as the great researchers of humanity such as Nikola Tesla, who achieved from his vision to try to transform a reality to massify the use of energy for free with his brilliant ideas through the use of an antenna that had global reach, so also the leadership of any institution has to demonstrate that it has a commitment to research to transform reality and make people both internal and external customers feel inspired to give the best of themselves and start dreaming of a reality that is optimal and that contributes to the welfare of all individuals who make up the University community.

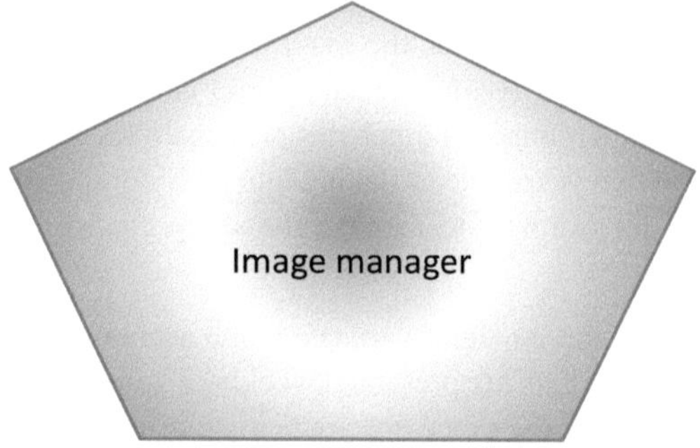

Source: Correa O, 2024. Image manager.

It is important to point out that nowadays, in the educational processes oriented to data processing, image managers are also used, initially in the servers at the beginning of the 21st century, they worked with file managers that represented the opportunity to upload file by file all those contents supported by graphics that they wanted to manage to nourish the web pages or Internet sites that were being developed.

It is necessary to emphasize that in the second decade of the XXI century all this has been evolving in a vertiginous way, it has evolved from images that traditionally had a capacity based on a megabyte to images with great definition that can exceed up to 20 Mb.

In addition to this, there are now servers that have incorporated not only cloud technology in terms of almost infinite storage, but also the possibility for the user to enter an introduction or phrase that refers to a specific topic and obtain as a result an image or video that can be hosted on the site where the user is interacting in real time.

Based on this principle, it is necessary to point out that all these systems are nowadays connected to the so-called intelligent learning, where the system interacts with a user simultaneously to generate learning that is shared and serves as an experience to approach new knowledge topics.

Now, all this is based on devices that have been developed taking into consideration the brain, specifically the neurons that form a fundamental part of our reasoning. Obviously, the human being has become the fundamental element to be studied in order to develop the new machines that are required to respond efficiently to the technological developments that are currently being developed.

That is why reference is made to neural learning, in which definitely in the case of computers today is based on the so-called neural processors also known as NPU. In this sense it is necessary to emphasize that the logical structure of this processor takes into consideration the structure of neuronal relationships of the human being, but today with the development of mathematical models based on variables and vectors, this can be applied in a practical way to solve problems of daily life.

In this construction of matrices there are multiple relationships that at any given time may generate an error, but it also has the ability to amend it in such a way that, although they do not show emotions like those of human beings, they have full practical awareness that they can improve to the extent that they interpret new interruptions and give results to new objectives set.

In the case of human beings it is often observed that there are multiple interactions to generate a final result. This is very evident in the case of research when a researcher being in South America can have contact with various researchers in different continents to apply a survey that leads to reliable results on a research topic that is being developed either at a social level or that has to do with the scientific field.

It is paradoxical to point out that once the researcher has obtained his results, he proceeds to publish them in a scientific journal of international scope, which will allow the generation of new knowledge from those professionals who will have access to the article, but will also have the ability to relate them to new topics.

In this way it can be observed that a series of relationships are traced today at a global level in an investigative topic, with the passage of time it joins new investigations to recreate previous knowledge and try to generate new concepts that adapt to the changing technological reality.

In the case of neural processors, they work with matrices, which can generate multiple interactions between them in order to evaluate a specific subject, and when compared in a matter of seconds with other dimensions or variables, they can reconstruct a new design according to the requirements demanded by the user in the field of artificial intelligence.

It is necessary to indicate that this type of neural processors in the next decade will have a high-level applicability, since it can be incorporated in laptops, Tablet computers and smart cell phones. It should be taken into consideration a basic principle such as navigation which today already allows the user to have a synthesis or result generated by artificial intelligence, which allows synthesizing the result of the search in a way that covers the global whole to try to bring the end user the maximum level of functionality to what he wants at this time.

It is necessary to understand that, in the next operating systems, the tendency to incorporate programs based on artificial intelligence will be greater every day, therefore, surely technologies will be developed that based on motherboards that are coupled to the so-called NPU will allow the end user to have a greater benefit and approach to those programs based on artificial intelligence that have been overcoming traditional forms of search on the Internet.

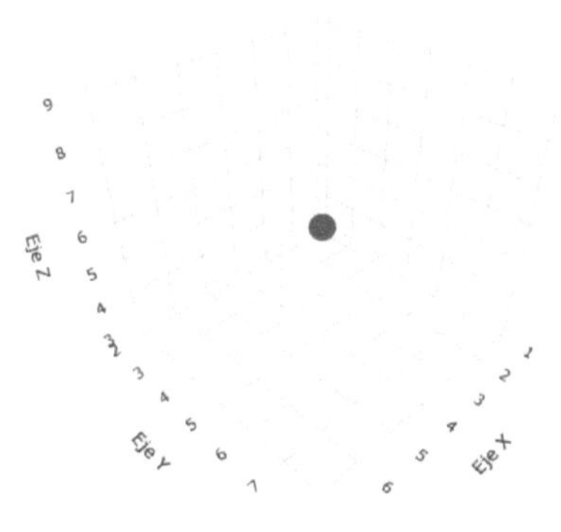

Source: Correa O, 2024. Data processing indicators.

Analyzing data processors in terms of search engines in the coming years there will surely be an increase in the use of artificial intelligence to obtain search results. The tendency is to try to give a summary of what you want to find by generating a first link that has been the result of the comparison analysis interpretation of what would represent what a user really wants to find.

In the past, a ranking from 1 to 10 could be observed, and in theory the first numbers represented the best search options; however, the neural analysis of these search engines nowadays focuses on giving a single result that is relevant and that generates a practical utility for the user who is looking for a specific content.

It is necessary to indicate that, if this continues to evolve towards processes based on artificial intelligence, then the video and image editing programs, surely incorporated in the operating systems, will also allow the user to generate a new image from a text or phrase that he wishes to incorporate in his design, which will surely also be highly useful for the generation of video and multimedia content in general.

Obviously, in the context of this situation, one of the guidelines that the user should have in the coming years when acquiring a computer is to verify that it contains a neural processing unit, which will allow greater functionality when using this type of resources.

In the case of word processing programs, you will surely see that they will include the option of the list, in which it will no longer be necessary as before to make a previous practice for the program to incorporate the tone of voice to the database, but surely they will become so direct that simply from the first dictation they will recognize the word that you want to reveal, surely they will have the ability to make some kind of suggestion regarding for example the content that is being written, how to write it and what elements of current events can be incorporated.

This does not mean at all that artificial intelligence is surpassing the capabilities of human beings, but simply that all these processes will come for people to have greater breadth when making their writing or documents, it will surely remain an additional tool that people can use in this regard to have additional ideas or updated approaches incorporated into the text editing processes that are at some point running.

Surely in the future we will see presentation editing programs in which you simply enter the topic you want to develop, and artificial intelligence will allow the user to choose a series of images or videos that come to support each of the ideas that you are trying to capture in each of the slides.

Definitely the use of the so-called virtual reality will be enhanced with artificial intelligence, the lenses focused on the development of activity in these virtual worlds will surely be connected to these neural networks and will allow the user to select different worlds and establish what style of design or images they consider that may be relevant to their game or process they are performing with the use of their smart glasses that will surely be connected to the internet, to neural networks that will work in concordance with NPU processors, to recognize all the images that are presented, improve them and surely create more advanced levels according to the expectations of each user.

So surely if at this moment there is a sense of surprise or amazement, in the next 20 years we will see the possibility that each user with the use of neural networks can even create conversation groups in which they can establish specific topics, and they can give instructions of the images or videos they want to capture in real time to share with other people, which will definitely be of great importance when it comes to establish debates in real time on television stations or in the direct of the different social networks of planet earth, this will ensure that the interest of people to get involved in technologies and acquire these new computers will be something truly fascinating at a global level.

It is necessary to understand that nowadays artificial intelligence has the ability to make mathematical predictions about possible situations that may occur in the future. For example, if you want to know the possibility of building a space base on the planet Mars, obviously the neural systems through artificial intelligence programs will generate as a result images, videos and texts taking into consideration the latest technologies that are currently available in terms of space travel.

 For example, the possibility of potentiating a tesla coil to generate a space travel process, taking into consideration, for example, the current advances in particle colliders, which already allow us to have an idea that approximately by the year 2050 the realization of space travel to Mars will be something that will have powerfully consolidated humanity.

By the year 2050, the generation of results and searches based on artificial intelligence will be of great use in the establishment of spatial bases, since it will allow scientists to recognize in real time the characteristics of a specific terrain and how a material was previously applied and what results can be obtained in a given atmospheric situation.

So simply those procedures of taking a sample and taking it to a laboratory to analyze the chemical or biological components of a certain material will be surpassed to the extent that research incorporates image recognition based on artificial intelligence, which definitely with the current libraries that are available will be able to perform analysis quickly to determine the biological or mineral chemical components of a material that can be found on another planet.

From this analysis, scientists will also be able to simulate the scenario in time and space of the application of a specific material in certain conditions on another planet. This will contribute significantly to improve the scientific process that traditionally on earth is known as trial and error, and although it is true that through a process of continuous improvement great results can be achieved, it is also necessary to say that in uncertain scenarios, sometimes it is not possible to invest so much time but optimal and faster results are required in order to provide answers to the needs that must be immediately solved.

Source: Correa O, 2024. Data visualization.

By visualizing data, today thanks to artificial intelligence, people involved in household tasks can begin to generate science and obtain scientific results within their field of action. So, for example, a traditional activity such as planting a tree or weeding a yard can become an amazing scientific experience that dazzles the whole world.

It is necessary to emphasize that for example a gardener empowered with an artificial intelligence phone and an image recognition program can begin to establish a database based on all those images he collects of the plants that are in his garden. Once collected, the artificial intelligence will be able to tell him the scientific name of each of those plants and their application.

So it can also be said that with the advent of artificial intelligence all trades will be resized to the point of becoming an activity of great scientific importance that can be transmitted globally through social networks, but also in some cases can be done formally through what is the generation of a scientific article that when published reveals for example the minerals or plants found in a garden and the possible uses of these resources.

At this point, every profession will become extremely exciting, a person who has a garden can have a database of images that can be uploaded to a server in the cloud, can process these images to determine the natural or biological chemical characteristics and thus be able to understand, for example, the application of these components in today's products.

For example, a person may find an aloe vera plant in his garden, and by taking a photo of it with an artificial intelligence recognition program, he will determine the beneficial uses of that plant in terms of personal hygiene, for example. At that point, everything that appeared to be an ornament or a complement in the garden could represent the opportunity to establish an investigation that has scientific characteristics to recognize everything that one has and what could be its uses.

Universities traditionally have a curricular unit linked to community service, in which they often try to generate an activity that is beneficial to the community, such as planting plants or simply giving a talk related to ethics and values in community coexistence.

Now surely with the advent of artificial intelligence this wonderful curricular unit of the university will be enhanced, because with the use of intelligent technology students will be able to recognize the existing elements in a given space, what are their properties and possible uses that lead them to improve their community.

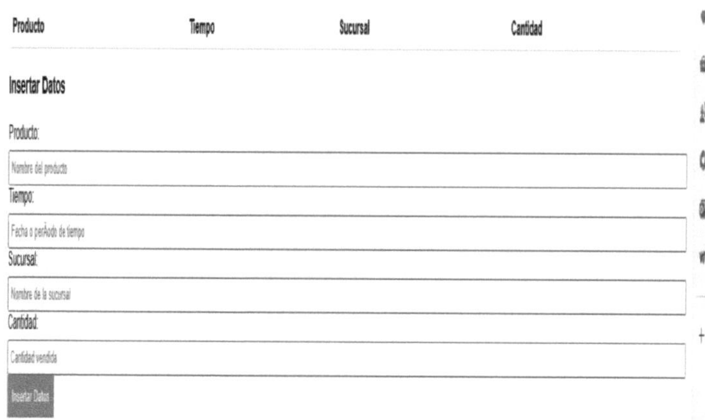

Source: Correa O, 2024. Database in 3 dimensions.

In the field of medicine, new systems will surely begin to appear that, by taking a photo focused on a particular organ of the human body, can give an orientation as to its situation so that possible solutions will also arrive so that medical professionals can have sophisticated tools that allow them to make the appropriate diagnoses and therefore generate the solutions required for each patient.

Image recognition, object recognition and facial identification are definitely in their infancy, but surely these advances that are currently being developed will be the fundamental bases for new programs that can be applied in different fields of science.

Surely for situations related to appliance repairs, in the case of the blender, in the future they will surely be able to take a picture of the rotor and be able to determine the current state and surely the artificial intelligence will generate a recommendation to the technician who will try to improve the appliance, for example, so that it can be used with more power.

This will mean that people and companies that develop products will have to make their qualities based on quality, because those products that are of maximum performance and efficiency will surely be recommended by artificial intelligence systems and therefore will be the best sellers globally.

In this way it can be seen that those people or businesses that have hyper-specialized in a subject, can through the quality and proven use of their product have a global reach to ensure the sale of their products every day new markets.

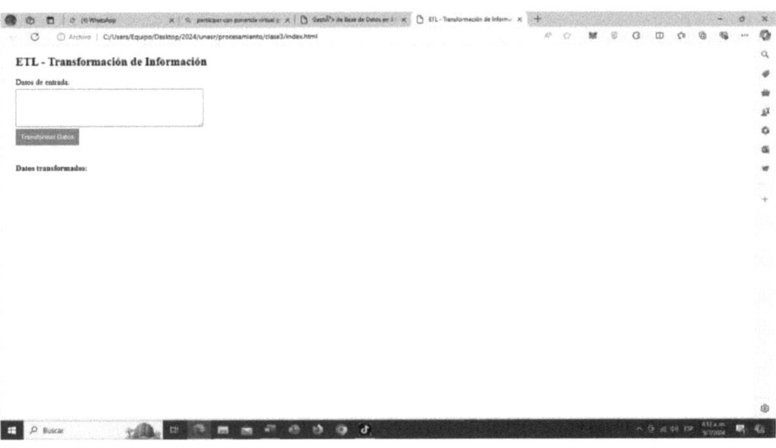

Source: Correa O, 2024. Information transformation.

In areas such as for example the decoration of the environments surely having a smartphone and a photo recognition program, the person in charge of improving an environment or make it more comfortable by taking a picture can analyze it under the perspective of artificial intelligence, for example, the Bagua map of ancestral visions such as feng shui that nowadays have been incorporated to the new environments, and whose vision is the harmonization of a certain place through the five elements of nature established in the philosophy and vision of life of feng shui.

Surely these systems will recognize the nine areas of the Bagua map, they can give a recommendation of some element that allows harmonizing for example the area of love in a certain room of the house, or simply if it is required to improve the economy surely the artificial intelligence will recommend in zone 1 of the map of the bedroom the room to incorporate for example the water element to make the economy more fluid in a certain home according to that ancestral Chinese philosophy.

For all these reasons it is evident that most professions will be enhanced with the incorporation of this type of technology systems, obviously to the extent that NPU processors are improving the processes and results will be greater to better substantiate each of the activities you want to express, therefore, in the best case we can see which traditional trades may begin to focus on continuous improvement.

Having not only clear the importance of the inspection, obtaining results of probable uses in different countries of the world in order to have a graphical or numerical vision of the application of a procedure, making historical analysis around a certain situation to say that every person who develops a trade implementing artificial intelligence with NPU processors and image recognition at first can be a leader in their community that will definitely take their process or productive activity to another higher level.

Source: Correa O, 2024. Social Network.

Definitely one of the characteristics of the implementation of artificial intelligence today in social networks, with the development of facial recognition is the chronological awareness of the individual. People today, for example, by focusing a camera on their face can go back 10 or 15 years in time to their adolescence or childhood.

To be able to remember past times, but also to have the possibility in the case of not having the photos of those times, to artificially recreate that important individual past that you can project in many cases through social networks to share with your friends or family.

But it is also relevant to point out in the case of social networks that already in the framework of facial recognition there is the possibility of using a webcam that allows the individual to project his image into the future as it will be seen in later years, obviously that artificial intelligence through facial recognition begins to add biological and physiological elements to the person to make him look of a certain age in the near or distant future.

In many social networks, it is even possible to see the possibility that a person through an artificial intelligence program, by using facial recognition, can determine particular emotional characteristics that he or she is going through at a certain moment, such as joy or enthusiasm, for example.

So by mentioning all these aspects, we begin to see that artificial intelligence, when used properly, begins to generate processes of self-awareness in the individual that allow him to generate that recognition, that projection into the future of what I am and what I want to become.

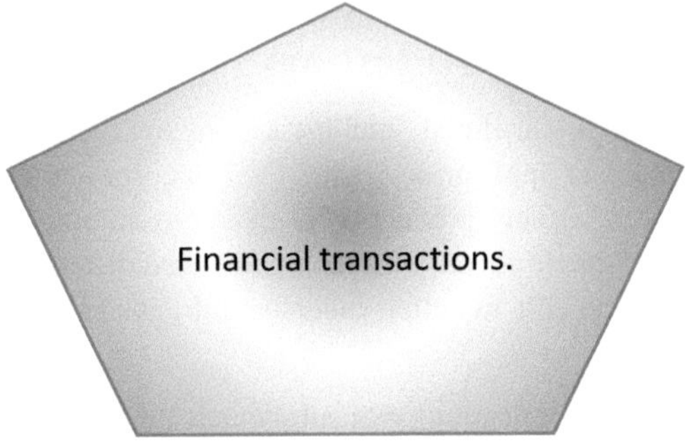

Source: Correa O, 2024. Financial transactions.

Definitely to the extent that in the next computers and smartphones integrate NPU processors, it will be possible to observe the analysis in real time of the different markets in the world, thus being able to draw a comprehensive analysis based on their performance in the last five years and what can be expected of such performance for the next 5 years.

At this point, artificial intelligence systems, including the most advanced neural processors, will definitely face a trial by fire because even if they can make an exhaustive analysis of the variations in the different shares or value of companies in previous years, it will be quite difficult for them to predict future behavior because new variables such as human behavior, climate change and the personal leadership of each individual, which in turn is based on genetics, personal, social and cultural factors, are involved.

Thus, people's leadership will continue to be at least in the next 20 years a fundamental factor in the management of companies and institutions, which can be enhanced with the use of these neural tools to support decision making at any given time.

Source: Correa O, 2024. APK Development.

With the implementation of artificial intelligence in the coming years will surely increase the development of applications, which will incorporate certain fundamental functions focused on certain new products. For example, intelligent cars, which will surely have better processors to identify routes, established distances and thus, through better voice recognition, be able to better understand the instructions that people wish to dictate to them.

In the case of automobiles, applications will surely arrive that will allow them to make an exhaustive analysis of the climatic situations in a given geographical area, in order to be able to drive autonomously towards a road that corresponds to a better weather condition to ensure the safety of all the people who are moving in this type of automated cars.

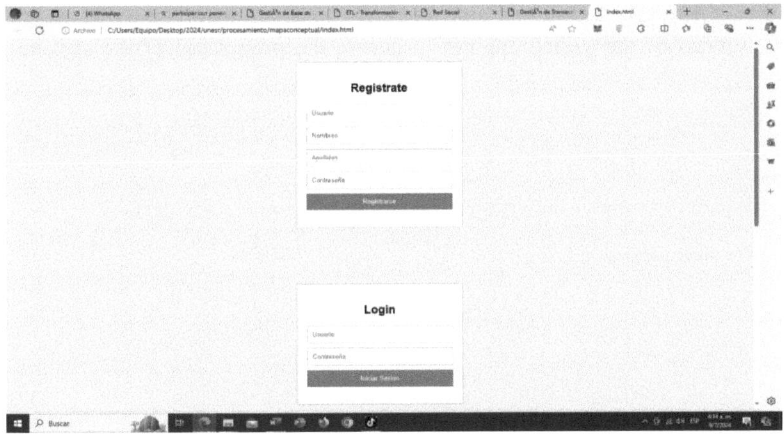

Source: Correa O, 2024. Registration and access.

In traditional applications, a one-to-one relationship is managed in terms of what is desired and what is obtained; the arrival of GPU processors increased the processing possibilities to develop programs based on artificial intelligence that represent new tools for people in their daily lives.

With the incorporation of NPU processors, the possibilities are increased because one instruction can generate 100 possible responses and those actions in turn can be interpreted 100 times more, which allows us in a short time to analyze more than 1000 possibilities around a specific topic.

In this sense, we can discern that artificial intelligence has the ability to learn based on the processes that are taking place, but it will also allow humans to have a better understanding of the processes it is studying and increase the possibilities of suggested solutions to a specific topic.

Certainly in issues related to access to international servers supported in the cloud, security options will increase, only the type of device from which you are trying to access, the IP address or region, operating system, but also the tone of voice and the speed of writing and expression of each person will be taken into consideration.

Such recognition patterns are currently visible in search engines when a person is transcribing information, and the search engine robots detect that there is an increase in the speed of transmission and immediately generate as a result the need for the user to give an answer or press a button to prove that he or she is really a human being.

Because many times machines are used to perform automated processes, in some cases so evaluating the speed of transcription nowadays with the use of the Internet is something that is demonstrated in real time and that can be an important indicator for the security systems of the search engines to ensure the proper use of the systems globally.

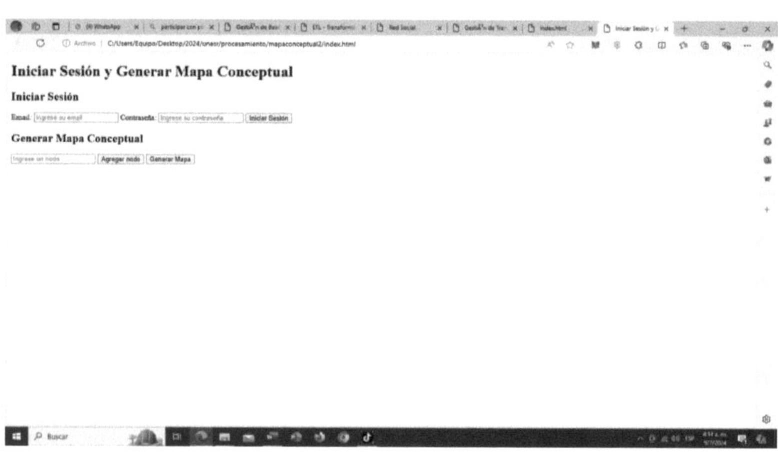

Source: Correa O, 2024. Log in.

Most of the Artificial Intelligence systems are currently going through a process of continuous improvement, in some cases each company establishes its policies and procedures what is acceptable, what is not to be accepted.

In the transit of this process many times users introduce syntaxes that may clash with the internal policies of the company, thus generating an error, however, they also have a built-in way to communicate with the staff in order to clarify any doubt or error that is being generated in the application of an intelligent system.

In the generation of processes linked to data processing, at the educational level, a concept map is always established that is related to a given topic. Nowadays, with the use of artificial intelligence systems, this activity has been enhanced, since instructions can be dictated to generate an image that is related to the educational content to be transmitted at some point in time.

Source: Correa O, 2024. Data processing.

In the case of making reference to the NPU it would obviously give images linked to intelligent learning neural processes, in that sense the student who is performing the activity can see graphically what he is trying to develop from the conceptual vision to have a better understanding of the situation.

From the graphic vision then try to build a new conception or a new vision taking into consideration what the student knows to be true in order to translate it directly into his concept map. At this point it is necessary to keep in mind that there are company names that resemble the activity that a student may be looking for.

This is observed especially in the field of electricity generation that have created cases in which companies have taken the name of the authors of the inventions and many times the results generated by the graphics come to be the logo of a company obviously at that time it is necessary to make a clarification to the image generation system of artificial intelligence to focus on the theoretical components of what you want to get.

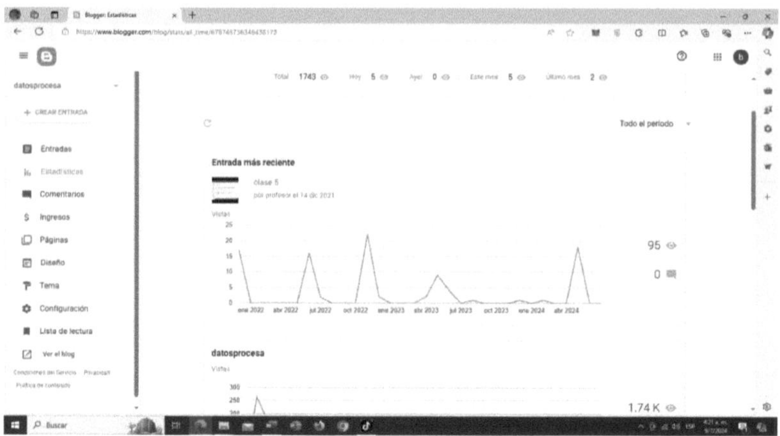

Source: https://datosprocesa.blogspot.com/ Tickets.

In terms of data processing, every day the teaching and learning processes are based on multimedia systems, and in that sense the processors will allow the participants of a specific curricular unit to obtain a text summary of what a video says either in the language being expressed or in another specific language, so that each person through the use of artificial intelligence can obtain a kind of dictation of each word that an author is specifically relating and that often is required to read to reaffirm with strength the understanding of the content that has been reported.

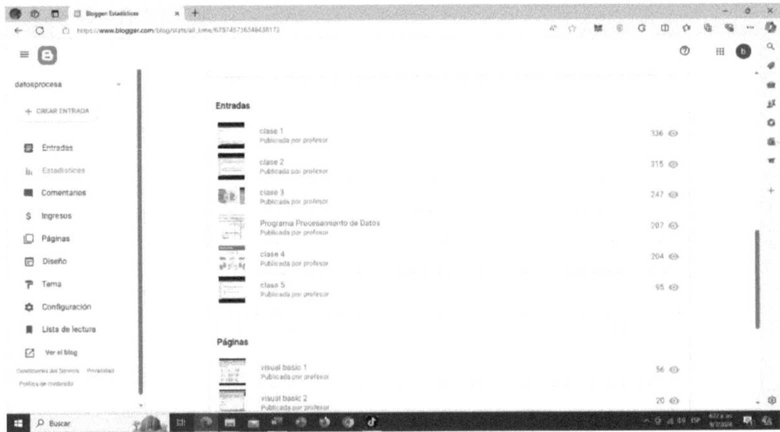

Source: https://datosprocesa.blogspot.com/ Classes.

Regarding data processing it is important to understand that artificial intelligence will be gaining more and more scenarios every day, it will surely have the ability to show many people not only its advantages but how it works internally how this algorithm is organized through matrices and three-dimensional graphics, so that people become aware of the matrix possibilities it has to build a new love a new element from the exponentiation in a second of 100 elements to 4, for example to be able to have a forecast of the time to take for 5 years taking a growth of 10% in the manufacturing industry, elements that at first may seem hypothetical but that in the real one allow to have solid arguments for example to recommend the planting of 1000 trees in each new productive process or community that is established, assuming the importance that this has for the natural development of human beings on earth.

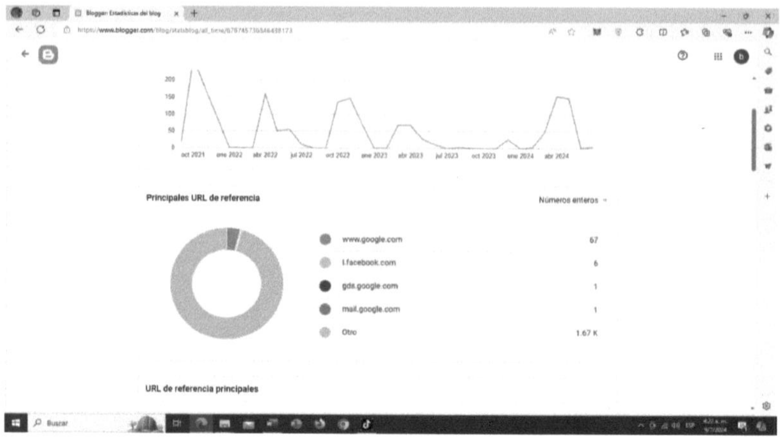

Source: https://datosprocesa.blogspot.com/ Reference URL.

Definitely when teaching a data processing course, it is necessary to understand the importance of incorporating the use of NPU processors into the educational process. For example, you can create case studies in which four new ventures are incorporated into a community, and thus be able to determine a projection of indicators in the time span of the next three months how could be the cognitive evolution of each of the participants in their interaction with the customer.

What could be the next strategies for incorporating technology and applications to ensure the quality of the services being provided. All these activities proposed as practical exercises will contribute to the affirmation of managerial leadership and entrepreneurial approach that every university student should have, which definitely the recent history of the XXI century showed that they are the ones who have the ability to empower themselves with technology and take it to a global scale to transform global processes involving humanity.

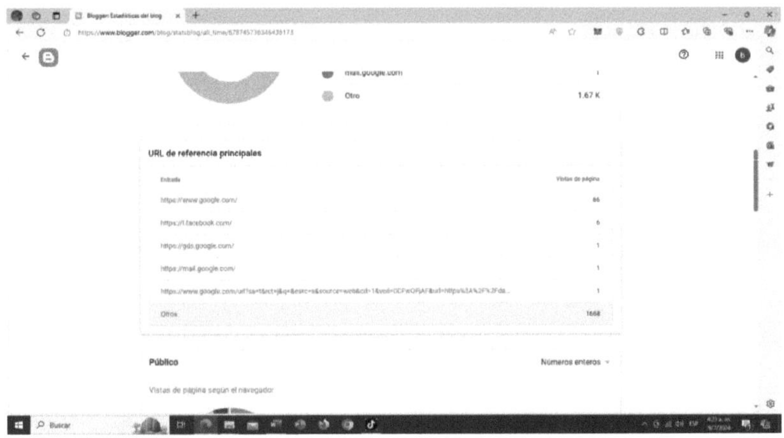

Source: https://datosprocesa.blogspot.com/ URL of main references.

Obviously it is necessary that all facilitators of the curricular unit linked to data processing, have basic fundamentals regarding CPU, GPU and NPU processors, in order to understand that they can generate new scenarios taking into consideration aspects of the past and its influence on the future, but above all, being aware that the University activity is fundamental for the development of society.

To understand that the person who has a smartphone in his hands today has the ability to scientifically discover the reality that surrounds him, but also to transform it positively taking into consideration the useful recommendations of artificial intelligence, but at the same time sowing awareness about the preservation of the natural environment that today sustains life on earth.

While it is true that in the course of these transcribed sentences it has been demonstrated that the human being has been the basis for the development of new neural technological processes, then it is extremely necessary to understand that the preservation of the current natural environments will allow humanity to continue generating science to develop technological processes much more advanced than those currently possessed.

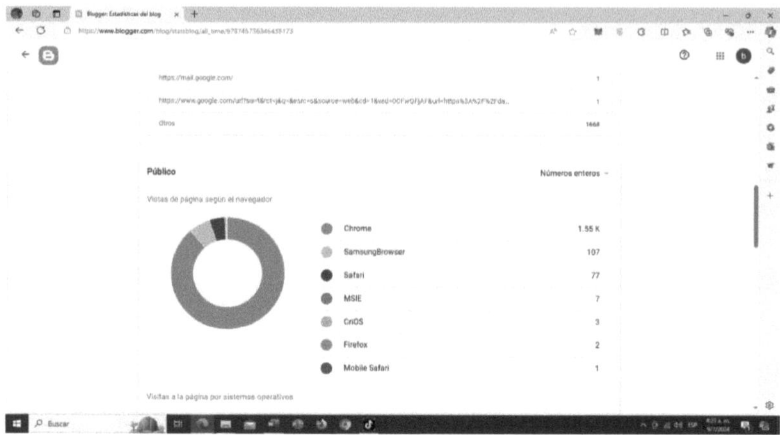

Source: https://datosprocesa.blogspot.com/ Browsers.

In a data processing unit where simply the use of artificial intelligence, tempted in NPU processors, definitely establish activities linked to the tree natural processes, and sustainability in each productive process can definitely be something that is represented either a mind map or in a graph that each student can capture to understand that going hand in hand with nature, can serve as inspiration to establish new technological models that contribute to have a global impact and therefore make much more productive.

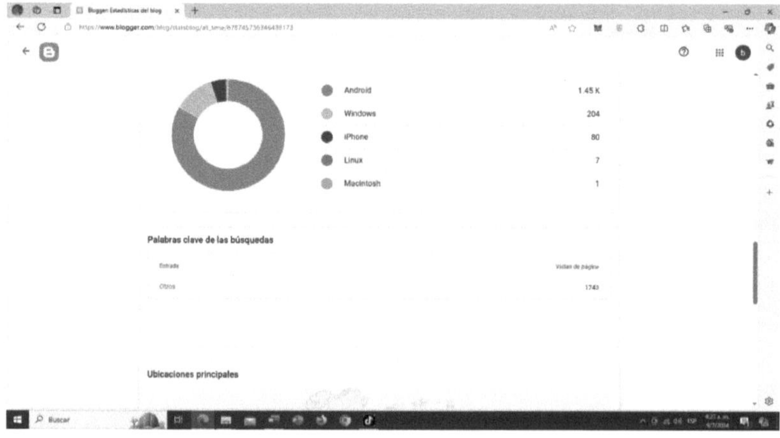

Source: https://datosprocesa.blogspot.com/ Operating Systems.

With the use of artificial intelligence in the framework of data processing, practical exercises can be established taking into consideration the undertakings of each student, so if a student has decided to create transistors to be incorporated into a GPU card, then he should also set as a goal how this technological device can strengthen the local ecosystems where he is generating his enterprise, to also become fully aware of the natural processes that take place in nature from the simplest as the germination of a seed to the most complex as evaporation, condensation and precipitation that occur in nature.

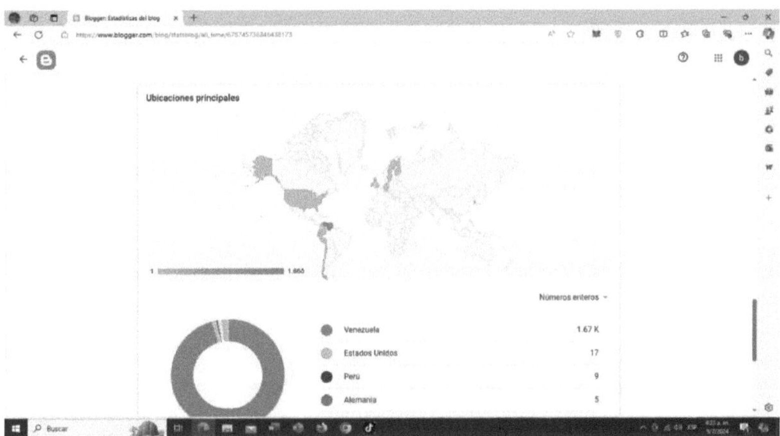

Source: https://datosprocesa.blogspot.com/ Countries.

With the use of artificial intelligence, it will be possible to establish planting plans for a certain number of trees, which will generate climatic stability in a given area. This type of activities can also contribute in the beginning as an example in the areas of mathematics, so that students can have full understanding of space and time, thus generating activities that are sustainable over the years and generate profitability, which is after all the indicator that is established globally as the fundamental basis of any company.

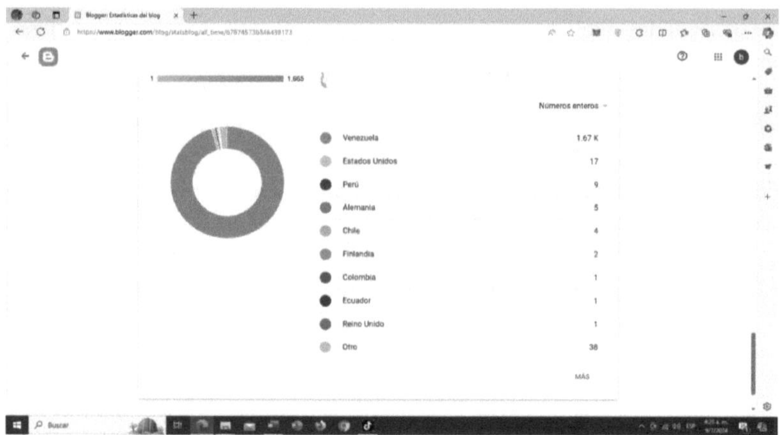

Source: https://datosprocesa.blogspot.com/ Countries.

Definitely one of the great lessons that come to bring all these advances based on neural processors, is that it is really worth spending time to mathematics that are present in nature, and how all that comes to generate a balance for the maintenance of life on earth.

All these changes sow hope for the reaffirmation of all professionals in their various careers, the case of teachers opens the door to establish new teaching models that take into consideration the technological changes, leading the participant to become aware of their reality and the opportunity they have to have intelligent technology to transform it in a sustainable way which becomes the real wealth for all humanity in general.

Bibliographic references.

Agenda 2030 and the Sustainable Development Goals. An opportunity for Latin America and the Caribbean. United Nations publication. United Nations, February 2017. All rights reserved. Printed in Santiago.LC/G.2681/Rev.1. S.17-00110

Arias, F. (2012) *El Proyecto de Investigación Introducción a la metodología científica.* Editorial Episteme 2012 6 edition. Available in electronic format (PDF) from the website: https://ebevidencia.com/wp-content/uploads/2014/12/EL-PROYECTO-DE-INVESTIGACI%C3%93N-6ta-Ed.-FIDIAS-G.-ARIAS.pdf [Accessed 2019, November 14].

World Summit on the Information Society. Geneva 2003 Tunis 2005. Document WSIS-03/GENEVA/4-E May 12, 2004.

Escobar, J. (2020) *Hard and soft technologies, and their consequences of their uses for the environment.* Available at: https://webcache.googleusercontent.com/search?q=cache:NGHtsQEbWkgJ:h ttps://liceopolitecnicoc52.jimdofree.com/app/download/6181688666/TECNOL OGIAS%2BDURAS%2BY%2BTECNOLOGIAS%2BBLANDAS_ABCE.pdf%3 Ft%3D1596483126%26mobile%3D1+&cd=1&hl=en-419&ct=clnk&gl=ve

Silva, Francisco (2010) Software libre y educación un estudio de casos en la enseñanza obligatoria en Cataluña. University of Barcelona, Faculty of Pedagogy. Available in electronic format (PDF) at the website: diposit.ub.edu/dspace/bitstream/2445/43114/2/Tesis_FACS.pdf.

Zálvez (2017) Analysis of OpenSource ICT resources to support students with NN.EE. in the environment of PBL methodologies. DOCTORAL PROGRAM INNOVATION AND RESEARCH IN DIDACTICS FACULTY OF EDUCATION DOCTORAL THESIS UNED. Available in electronic format (PDF) http://e-spacio.uned.es/fez/eserv/tesisuned:ED-Pg-InoInvDid-Jpzalvez/ZALVEZ_RICO_JuanPedro_Tesis.pdf [Accessed 2023, April 20].

Zanotti Agustin (2013) El software libre y el campo de producción cordobés: DOCTORADO EN ESTUDIOS SOCIALES DE AMÉRICA LATINA. UNIVERSIDAD NACIONAL DE CÓRDOBA CENTRO DE ESTUDIOS AVANZADOS. Available in electronic format (PDF) https://rdu.unc.edu.ar/bitstream/handle/11086/1408/El%20software%20libre%2 0y%20el%20campo%20de%20producci%c3%b3n%20cordob%c3%a9s%20.... pdf [Accessed 2023, April 20].

yes
I want morebooks!

Buy your books fast and straightforward online - at one of world's fastest growing online book stores! Environmentally sound due to Print-on-Demand technologies.

Buy your books online at
www.morebooks.shop

Kaufen Sie Ihre Bücher schnell und unkompliziert online – auf einer der am schnellsten wachsenden Buchhandelsplattformen weltweit! Dank Print-On-Demand umwelt- und ressourcenschonend produziert.

Bücher schneller online kaufen
www.morebooks.shop

info@omniscriptum.com
www.omniscriptum.com

Printed by Books on Demand GmbH, Norderstedt / Germany